THE JOURNEY TO BECOMING A NURSE

DR. TONYA DIXON

⫶D

DOCTOR DIXON PUBLICATIONS

For information contact:
DoctorTonyaDixon@gmail.com
The Consultants Circle
Book and Cover design by Dr. Tonya Dixon
@ Doctor-Dixon Publications & Educational Services
ISBN: 978-0-578-67531-2

First Edition: May 2020

❀ Created with Vellum

The Journey to Becoming A Nurse is dedicated to Thelma Rene Brown (my mother), Deceased, Never Forgotten. Thank you for birthing, loving, providing, supporting, and encouraging me in life and in nursing. Always with me in spirit. "The Wise Old Owl"

The Journey to Becoming A Nurse is also dedicated to all levels of nursing students and nurses. It is my hope that this work be shared. After all, when we share knowledge and experiences, we support and often encourage individual nurses along their journey.
Dr. Tonya Dixon

A journey of a thousand miles begins with one step.

CONTENTS

Part One
DR. DIXON'S TOOLBOX

INTRODUCTION

This book educates the reader about the many steps that it takes along the journey to becoming a nurse. The book is comprised of 8 chapters. Chapters 1-7 are topic specific. Each chapters provides, tips, strategies, and recommendations. Chapter 8 is the final chapter and provides a toolbox of references that may be helpful. A tribute to students follows.

Chapter 1- Step One: Researching

Researching nursing programs is of high importance. At the beginning of the the journey the perspective student is in the process of gathering information on programs that could result in a life changing decision. Chapter 1 provides recommendations that may aid in making the decision to become a future nurse.

Chapter 2- Step Two: Knowing

Knowledge about various items will help position the student. Either pre-entry or at the beginning of the program is a good time to learn about your individual needs and the program. In addition, it is a good time to develop strategies for success. Chapter 2 provides strategies to assist in being prepared.

Chapter 3- Step Three: Understanding

It is important to gain a thorough understanding of what is expected in the classroom, laboratory (skills), simulation, and clinical components of the nursing program. It is also important to understand what is expected as a student in the profession. Chapter 3 further describes components of a nursing program and provides tips on how to navigate as a nursing student.

Chapter 4- Step Four: Navigating

During this time, the student is in the trenches of the program and is preparing for the National Council Licensing Examination (NCLEX). This exam requires preparation and will test all of the knowledge learned in the program. Chapter 4 discusses NCLEX and provides tips and links.

Chapter 5- Step Five: Preparing

Preparing ones self for entry into the profession is key. Chapter 5 discusses resumes, portfolios, and interviews. Both of these tools are recommended and template and guidance on development is located in the final chapter.

Chapter 6- Step Six: Transitioning

After program and NCLEX completion there is a transition from student nurse to licensed nurse. This is a time to become acclimated in the professions of nursing, and apply newfound knowledge. Chapter 6 discusses transition to practice, preparation for independence, building bridges, establishing boundaries, and professional development.

Chapter 7- Step Seven: Becoming

During this time the licensed nurse is making key decisions as a member of the profession. The topics in chapter 7 includes a discussion on environments, maintaining composure, and discusses ways to avoid burnout.

Chapter 8- Dr. Dixon's Toolbox

Chapter 8, provides resources referenced throughout chapters 1-7. These may be helpful pre and post program. The book concludes with words of wisdom from the author, and a tribute to previous students.

PREFACE

The road to becoming a nurse is not an easy one. There are various struggles that those who pursue a career in nursing experience. I searched for a comprehensive book that discussed the struggles that occur along the journey to beaconing a nurse. However, I was unable to find one single book that discussed these struggles while providing tips, strategies, and recommendations to alleviate them.

The intent of this book is to help the aspiring student nurse, enrolled student nurse, newly licensed nurse, or professional nurse along the journey. My motivation for writing the book stemmed from being a 20 year member of the profession of nursing and 15 years spent as a nurse educator, director, supervisor, clinical instructor and professor. The writing began in 2017. Once I completed the doctorate in curriculum and instruction from Northern Illinois University I was compelled to complete the book. This is one of my contributions to the next generation of nurses. It is my hope that all readers enjoy some small piece of it.

Dr. Tonya Dixon Ed.D, MSN, MBA, MPH, RN

The Journey to Becoming A Nurse

A Step by Step Guide

DR. TONYA DIXON

If we knew what it was were doing.... It would not be called research, would it?

— ALBERT EINSTEIN

Chapter One

STEP ONE... RESEARCHING

Making the decision to become a nurse is one that should be taken seriously. Nursing programs are costly, takes time, dedication, and take a strong commitment to complete. There are many programs to choose from, options for degree levels, and various requirements for entry. It is important to research a program that will meet the individual students needs.

As I reflect on my search for a nursing program (nearly 30 years ago), I recall applying to four different programs. I was placed on a waiting list for all four. Nearly two and a half years later, I received two offers for admission. My strategy worked. I was excited about new possibilities. This chapter provides tips, strategies, and recommendations on things to consider when researching a nursing program.

THE NURSING PROFESSION
Becoming A Nurse Is The Reward

Nursing is a profession like no other. Nurses are caregivers, critical thinkers, patient advocates, and educators. Nurses bring comfort, stability, and a sense of well-being to individuals and families. Nurses are compassionate and caring. To be a nurse is an honor and a privilege.

The public holds nurses in high esteem. In fact, many Gallup polls results over the past decade recognize nurses as the most trusted among health care professionals. Nurses dedicate themselves to the service of others.

A career in nursing is a journey like no other. Each nurses journey is different. Individuals choose nursing for various reasons. That reason is typically never forgotten. If you have chosen the path of becoming a nurse, you have made a fantastic choice! Equip yourself with the knowledge needed to be the best.

"Welcome to nursing and the pursuits this journey entails. Your Journey begins here..."
Dr. Tonya Dixon

NURSING- ENTRY LEVEL

Nursing programs have various degree options. Three levels lead to initial nursing licensure. These include the licensed practical nurse (LPN); the associate degree nurse (ADN); and the bachelor of science in nursing (BSN). Below you will find the various entry levels, typical work places, and average program completion time.

Licensed/Practical Nurse (Certificate)- The LPN is a certificate program. LPN's work under the supervision of the RN. Many LPN's work in community-based agencies such as clinics, long term care, rehab, and doctors' offices. (1 Year)

Registered Nurse- (Associates Degree)- The Associate Degree in Nursing (ADN) is the minimum requirement for becoming a Registered Nurse (RN). The associate degree nurse works in community-based centers, acute care centers, and some work in corporate positions. (18-24 Months)

Registered Nurse- (Bachelors Degree) - The BSN is the recommended level of education for professional nursing. Upon completion the graduate is eligible for license. The BSN also awards the nurse who completes this degree with more autonomy in various roles. (Accelerated- 3 Years or Traditional- 4 Years).

NURSING- ADVANCED LEVEL

There are several advanced practice degrees and/or certifications. These are considered masters and post-masters programs. These programs vary in length. In fact, admission and completion depends on previous education and experience.

There are several ways that a student may be accepted into a nursing program. Some require previous degrees in nursing and others may provide an opportunity for students with degrees in other areas (besides nursing) to complete the advanced degree. In fact, many colleges and universities offer bridge programs to "bridge" or "seamlessly transition" the student to the next step. These programs have become increasingly popular over the last few years.

Masters Degree in Nursing (MSN)- The master's degree in nursing is a graduate program designed for those who want to practice in a specialized role or as an advanced practice registered nurse (APRN). (15 months- 2 Years)

Post Masters Programs: The post masters programs are pathways for nurses who have earned a master's degree and now wish to gain specialized knowledge in a specific area of concentration. Post masters programs may also help the nurse cross over into a different specialty than what they focused on in their masters program. A variety of programs are available. Below you will find the post masters program type, a small role description, and average completion times.

Nurse Practitioners (NP) are required (in some states) to work under the supervision of a physician. NPs have responsibility for diagnosing and treating. (18-24 months)

Clinical Nurse Specialists (CNS) shave advanced training and education in a specific patient group. These may be defined by a specific population, disease, type of care or the environment. (18-24 months)

Certified Nurse Midwives (CNM)s works with mothers during birth and post-partum. Certified Nurse Midwives are considered primary providers in all 50 states. CNS may be certified or licensed (2 years plus education)

Certified Nurse Anesthetist (CRNA) The CRNA administers anesthesia prior to procedures, monitors during surgery, oversees recovery, and develops plans for pain management. Some hospitals require nurse anesthetists to attain a doctoral degree. (2-3 years)

Doctoral Degrees: The doctoral degree in nursing is the highest level achievable in the field. Doctoral degrees build off of the masters level degree. The doctorate in nursing practice is a clinical nursing degree and the PhD is a research focused degree.

Doctorate of Nursing Practice (DNP)- The Doctor of Nursing Practice (DNP) is a doctoral degree and earns the graduate of a DNP program the title of doctorate. The DNP is a clinical practice degree. However, many scholars do not consider the DNP a terminal degree. (2-6 Years)

PHD in Nursing- (PhD) The PhD in nursing is a doctoral degree that is focused on research. Many consider the PhD a terminal degree. (2-6 years)

WHY NURSING?

Why Nursing? There are several reasons and benefits for joining the profession of nursing. First, there are various degree options. Second, there is flexibility in scheduling. Finally, there are a wide variety of settings in which a nurse may choose to work. Each of these provides opportunities for change and growth within the profession.

Degree Options: Varied degree/program options are available. This allows the nurse to have choice and flexibility in his/her education. Certificate, associates, bachelors, masters, post masters certificate, and doctoral programs are available.

Flexibility: There is flexibility in scheduling and roles. Nurses may work 4, 8, 10, 12-hour shifts, or as needed (prn). Schedules may be flexed around lifestyle. The possibilities are endless. Nurses may have roles as staff nurses, managers, administrators, practitioners, educators, faculty, clinical instructors, and/or researchers.

Variety of Settings: Nurses work in a variety of settings. Options include 1) community- such as clinics, doctors offices or as a school nurse; 2) Acute Care hospitals on a variety of specialty units; and 3) Corporate jobs and/or branches of the military to name a few.

ADMISSION REQUIREMENTS

Nursing programs have various admission requirements. Many of the requirements must be met prior to full consideration for admission. Other items may be met within certain time frames. Although each program is different, you will most likely need the following:

- Admission application/Admission/Processing fees
- Official Transcripts (Education)
- Standardized test scores/Entry exam scores
- Attend an Information Session
- Completion of an interview
- Letters of recommendation
- Resume (Work history) *health care a plus
- Certifications (CPR/BLS)

Tip: Pay attention to admission deadlines

DO I NEED EXPERIENCE?

Previous experience in healthcare is not required in all programs. However, healthcare experience gives you an advantage. It can also provide a good way to determine if healthcare is a good fit! There are a variety of roles that may increase knowledge, experience and exposure.

Roles:

- Become a certified nursing assistant, patient care tech
- Seek a job in the field (clinic, rehab, hospital)
- Volunteer at a health care institution
- Provide community service

Experience helps in the following ways:

- Understand the dynamics of healthcare
- Provides exposure to the realities of practice
- Communicate with patients and/or families
- Interact with members of the health care team
- Familiarity with roles and responsibilities
- Gain healthcare skills/Enhance hands-on abilities

HOW DO I FIND A PROGRAM?

Selecting the right program is probably one of the most important decisions for a future nursing student. There are many programs across the United States to choose from. The program you choose should meet your learning needs, be affordable, align with projected completion time, and prepare the graduate for success in the profession.

Adequate programs should maintain certain standards. Those standards include the following: 1) an ideal learning environment, 2) rigorous curriculum, 3) adequate support services, 4) timely completion rates, and 5) be fully accredited. These types of program have often been around for some time, has community partnerships, and have an excellent reputation within the profession.

Tip: Creating a search strategy for a reputable program is key to success!

Tool: Free Search Strategy Tool in Dr. Dixon's Toolbox

THINGS TO CONSIDER

Below are important considerations for program selection.

Accreditation: Assess if program is accredited.

Reputation: Research reputation and NCLEX pass rates.

Time: Look at completion time and consider program intensity (scheduling).

Education Models: Determine if the program is face to face (on-site); hybrid (virtual and on-site); on-line with self selection for clinical education; or a combination.

Support Services: Ask about tutoring, financial aid, scholarships, and job placement.

Financial Cost: Consider tuition, books, fees, extra costs.

Program: Assess the program. How are classes/courses offered? Request an information packet (these often detail admission requirements, deadlines, and program overview). Consider touring the campus.

Tip: Conduct an online search, weigh the Pros/Cons

Tool: Free Nursing Program Search Tool in Dr. Dixon's Toolbox

NURSING PROGRAM COST

Nursing programs vary in cost. Nursing tuition may be based on a semester, quarter, or an annual basis. The tuition reflects the normal time to complete. For example: A bachelor's degree in 2020 ranges from $40,000-100,000 at private and/or large universities. The costs is typically lower at a community college. Application, books and fees may also be separate. Tuition and fees are subject to change.

Financing Options:

- Cash/Personal Loans/Student Loans
- Federal government: federal financial aid is available to those who qualify. To apply log onto: Student Aid
- Grants/Loans: The U.S. Department of Education offers grants and loans
- Work study
- Scholarships
- Employer reimbursements

Tip: Check your institution for additional resources for financing your education.

WEIGHING THE PROS AND CONS

Making the Final Decision

Congratulations! Chances are if you are reading this, you have a decision to make. Now that you have an offer, you need to complete a program comparison. Make sure the program you select meets your needs and goals. The following are items to consider.

Program Offerings:

- Cost/Completion Time/Support
- Structure (Face to Face/Online/Hybrid)

Accreditation:

- Is the college or university reputable?
- Is the program accredited? (national or regional)

Pass Rates/Program Standing:

- What are first time NCLEX pass rates?
- What is program completion rate?
- Is the program on probation?
- Administrative warning for low pass rates?

APPLYING & PRE-ENTRY EXAMS

Applying: Applying to nursing programs requires planning. Acceptance to programs is competitive. Nursing schools have deadlines for admission and specific admission requirements. Many programs have waiting lists.

Plan your work and work your plan. Submit an accurate and complete application and monitor deadlines. While you are waiting to get accepted, continue working towards the end goal. Take some required courses, get ahead of the game.

Pre-Entry Exams: Often there is some sort of pre-entry exam that is required. It is a good idea to plan a review before your exam. Review books/study guides are available on Amazon or by conducting a Google search.

Possible Entry Exams: RN Cat, National League for Nursing Pre-Admission Exam (NLN PAX), Test of Essential Academic Skills (TEAS), Health Occupations Basic Entrance Exam (HOBET).

Tip: Apply to several programs.

Tool: Free Program search tool in Dr. Dixon's Toolbox

Sometimes it takes a good fall to know where you stand.

— HAYLEY WILLIAMS

Chapter Two

STEP TWO....KNOWING

Preparing for learning in a nursing program can be overwhelming. Nursing is a profession like no other and the education is rigorous. As a nurse you play a significant role in health care. In today's society nurses are considered the most trusted among healthcare professionals. The role of the nurse is vital and knowledge of the role is imperative.

As a future member of the nursing profession knowledge is power. Knowledge prepares "the nurse" for what lies ahead. It is important to know thy self. Take it from me, a major component of nursing education is dedication, knowing how to plan, organize, and what to expect. Assessing your own knowledge, how you learn, and your needs as a student will assist you become prepared for your program as well as for professional practice. This chapter provides tips, strategies, and recommendations on items you need to know.

STUDENT POPULATION

Nursing programs have a diverse student population. Students come with various backgrounds, education, age, skills set, and experiences. Students may be traditional or non-traditional. Nursing students work well together regardless.

The Traditional Student:

- Earns a high school diploma
- Enrolls immediately after high school.
- Usually a dependent
- Either works part time or not at all

The Non-Traditional Student:

- Experience delayed enrollment
- Attends part time for at least part of the year
- Works full time while enrolled 35 + hours
- Is financially independent
- Has dependents other than a spouse
- Is a single parent
- Does not have a traditional high school diploma (GED, or certificate)

PREPPING FOR THE FIRST DAY

The first day of nursing school can be overwhelming. You may be excited, curious, feel disorganized, and you may feel overwhelmed. Nutrition, comfort and preparedness is key.

Ensure you have adequate nutrition. Pack a nutritious meal or snack. Bring some water. Remember to hydrate.

Dress for comfort. Dress professional yet comfortable. Dressing in layers is a good idea because you don't know the temperatures for the locations you will be in. Get into the habit of wearing comfortable shoes.

Be prepared. Have your supplies (paper, pen, highlighter/book). Arrive early and be attentive. Take notes you can utilize a journal, notebook, I-Pad, tablet, or computer. If recording is permitted, record.

Tip: Early is On Time, On Time is Late, and Late is Unacceptable- Unknown Author

KNOWING YOUR LEARNING STYLE

We all learn differently. Being different is not a weakness. The key to effective learning is discovering your learning style and setting learning goals.

Three Primary Types of Learners: 1) *Auditory*- learn through hearing (record lectures); 2) *Visual*- learn by seeing and/or observing (watching videos, rewriting notes); and 3) *Kinesthetic*- learn from doing, writing or being hands on (repeat what you have learned).

Learning Goals: Once you have determined how you best learn you need to set learning goals. Learning goals can be set by creating timelines for both the long and short term. When setting learning goals you need to consider your program. Goals should be in alignment with program goals.

Tip: Consider how you best learn, that is your learning style.

DEVELOPING STUDY SKILLS

Study skills are critical in nursing. It is important to build excellent study skills. Study skills include organizing, managing your time, and knowing expectations.

Organizing options include the use of post its, flags, colored pens, pencils, highlighters, markers, colored paper, index cards, electronic documentation, files and folders.

Time Management is a huge component of developing study skills. Implementing proper study time is probably the most significant. One great way to manage study time is by creating a study calendar and committing to that study time.

Expectations include knowledge of the syllabus as well as and understanding of the grading, attendance, and exam policies. In an effort to know how you are being evaluated and/or assessed it is a good idea to review rubrics. Rubrics can be used as guideline to position yourself.

Tool: A sample study calendar is in Dr. Dixon's Toolbox

IMPLEMENTING STUDY STRATEGIES

There are several ways to implement study strategies. Paying attention, allowing group think, and establishing review strategies is helpful. Establishing, developing, and maintaining study strategies are key to learning as a nursing student. Recommended strategies are provided below.

Attention:

- Attend lectures/Stay focused
- Be attentive- Avoid distractions (phone, text)
- Take notes

Group Think:

- Develop study groups/ talk to others
- Create one to ones/brainstorm with others

Review:

- Power Points/Videos/Handouts
- Supplemental materials

THE NURSING PROCESS

The nursing process is a systematic way to collect and analyze data. The nurse utilizes the nursing process to make clinical decisions (reasoning). The nursing process involves five steps: assessment, diagnosis, planning, implementation and evaluation. The nursing process has been used for decades and really lays out a plan for how nurses plan and deliver care.

Assessment- The nurse collect and analyze data

Diagnosis- The nurse uses data to detect patients response to an actual or potential health needs or conditions

Planning- The nurse will set goals both short and long term

Implementation- The nurse carries out the plan of care

Evaluation- The nurse reviews the patients status for effectiveness, this happens continuously

The Nursing Process may be reviewed here.

Tip: Become familiar with the nursing process.

INTRODUCING THE CONCEPT MAP

Concept maps have proven to be great study tools. Completing the maps increases the ability for a student to link key concepts. Linking of information is beneficial as the concepts within the map helps the student nurse to understand the disease/disorder. The concept map includes 6 major components: five are on the disease in general. The sixth component allows the student to consider history and risk factors then compare the data to an actual patient (if comparing to a clinical patient).

- 1. Disease Name and Pathophysiology
- 2. Typical signs and symptoms
- 3. How disease/disorder is diagnosed (labs/tests)
- 4. Medical Treatment and/or Interventions
- 5. Nursing Treatment and/or Interventions
- 6. Patient Presentation (history/risk factors)

I encourage students to use concept maps as a study tool to link concepts within diseases/disorders. These may be used as a study tool for class or for clinical.

Tool: Concept Map Template located in Dr. Dixon's Toolbox

CONCEPT MAP CROSS-LINKS

Once you have decided to develop concept maps on the primary diseases/disorders they can be used to further advance your knowledge. The best way to utilize them is to complete each of the components (boxes). Then review the content by thinking across the various components of the map (cross-links). Cross-links help us to see how the information represented on the map are related to each other. How are these components linked? What are the relationships? Make these comparisons or **cross-links**:

- Does the disease patho match the typical symptoms?
- Does the treatment match the symptoms?
- Does the labs match the diagnosis or symptoms?
- Do the nursing interventions match the medical management?
- Do the tests/labs correlate with the pathophysiology?
- Does the patient presentation or history match the expected signs and symptoms ?

CONCEPT MAP EXEMPLAR DISEASES

Consider completing a concept map book. The idea is to cover major diseases that correlate with the diseases/disorders that are in your course of study. Previous students have created books, used the maps for studying, or created them in clinical. Utilize the list in any way you see fit.

I have created a sample of some of the diseases that may be categorized which is primarily organized by organ systems and has some other categories. This list is not exhaustive. It is simply a good "rough" of primary diseases/disorders. Students that I have encouraged to complete these have indicated that this is a good way to put the pieces together.

Tool: A Concept Map Exemplar is provided in Dr. Dixon's Toolbox

THE POWER OF THE TEXTBOOK

The textbook usually provides more depth than what is covered in lecture. Organize your notes, thoughts, and decipher key points. Write your thoughts out – determine what you know.

The Textbook:

- Please open and read the textbook
- The textbook provides depth of knowledge
- Reading the textbook adds clarity to lecture
- Assists in developing lab, simulation, and clinical knowledge

Other Learning Tools:

- Nursing Mnemonics (memory)
- NCLEX-styled questions (approach)
- Review of content (depth of knowledge)
- Concept maps (linking of concepts)
- Nursing case studies (application of knowledge)
- Pinterest nursing student tools (other strategies)

Tool: Free Concept Map Template in Dr. Dixon's Toolbox

GROUP WORK & STUDY BUDDY

There are several reasons to consider a study buddy. Group work is often required in nursing programs. As a member of the profession you will work with others. Research indicates that your chances of success are greater with a study buddy.

Why A Study Buddy?

- Two heads are better than one (combined knowledge)
- Learn how others study (increase study skills)
- Peer teaching (feedback from other)
- Motivate each other (support)
- Keep each other on task (organizing/planning)
- Keep you on track (accountability)
- Discussions (verbalizing ideas/thoughts)
- Opportunity to complete self-developed quiz
- Share experiences and resources
- Take note of various approaches to concepts

Tip: A study buddy allows you to see knowledge gaps. Try it.

WHAT ABOUT THE INSTRUCTORS?

Nursing instructors are committed to preparing the next generation of nurses. Contrary to popular belief nursing instructors are not the enemy! If you are curious about the instructor search for bios on the college/university website. Set up an office visit to make a connection.

Please know that instructors have an important role. The instructor organizes and plans all learning; mentors, advises, provides feedback; grades, evaluates, and assesses learning. Nursing instructors may be full or par time.

Nursing instructors are academically prepared and professionally committed. Their educational preparation typically includes a masters degree in nursing and have years of experience. Nursing instructors maintain lifelong learning through professional development and advanced education.

Tip: Instructors motivate. They are not the enemy.

PLANNING & ORGANIZING

Planning and organizing are critical for the nursing student. Students should institute good organizing and planning skills. There are items that are expected for the nursing student to know.

Plan on Reviewing the Following:

- Syllabus/Course Expectations/Course Objectives
- Grading Rubrics/Assignments/Grade Calculations
- Due Dates/Exam/Quiz Dates
- Attendance, Absence, and Exam policies

The nursing student should plan and organize their time. Students should not commit to any events, parties, travel, or vacation if it conflicts with your education. Time management is huge a calendar can help with this.

Tip: Create a calendar and use it for planning and organizing.

TOP TWELVE NURSING MUST HAVES

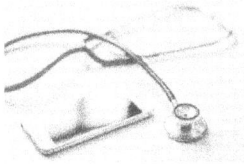

There are many items that can assist all nurses in the delivery of excellent nursing care. These items vary in style. Each item should be your choice. Top twelve include:

- Stethoscope
- Penlight
- Bandage Scissors
- Hemostats
- Collapsible clipboard
- Hand sanitizer
- Hand cream/lotion
- Cheat Sheets (with necessary info)
- Comfortable Shoes
- Watch with a second hand
- Organized tool for getting report (tracking sheet)
- Good pen

Nothing in life is to be feared... It is only to be understood.

— MARIE CURIE

Chapter Three

STEP THREE...UNDERSTANDING

Entry into the nursing profession requires a thorough understanding of the program. In fact, understanding the program is a critical step in nursing program success. Knowledge of program structure, expectations, and what to expect from day to day is important in nursing.

Nursing education is not like previously taken high school or college courses. Nursing courses and programs of study assess and develop knowledge, skills, and abilities. These skills are expected to build as the student moves through the program. There are various components of a nursing program. This section provides an overview of the various components and provides tips, and strategies that may be used for success.

WHAT IS THE PROGRAM LIKE?

Each nursing program is different. However, they typically have four major components that are similar across the nation: classroom, laboratory, simulation, and clinical. Nursing programs also cover different content. In addition, programs vary in the way that the course content is delivered. The manner in which courses are delivered should be discussed prior to admission into a program.

Nursing programs have broad as well as specific topics that will be developed and assessed. These topics are intertwined within the nursing program. These broad expectations include communication, professionalism, safety, and critical thinking. The next sections discuss each of these program components and topics.

Tip: Review your program and understand expectations.

CLASSROOM (THEORY) LEARNING

Classroom learning is where students receive theoretical content regarding major topics or concepts. This learning is often referred to as lecture or didactics. This may be delivered in a classroom setting (face to face) or in an online environment. In the classroom (theory) portion of the nursing program students are prepared for the National Council Licensing Examination (NCLEX).

Classroom learning is foundational and is what builds nursing knowledge. Many of the concepts covered in a nursing program includes areas which are often seen in practice. Classrooms and lecture sizes vary.

Facilitation may be strictly lecture or may involve group activities. The content delivered sets a foundation for exam knowledge. Nursing students cannot assume that the instructor is the sole designator of information, the nursing student has a responsibility to study the content.

PREPARING FOR EXAMS!

All students, particularly nursing students need to understand the basic rule of thumb for studying. For every 1 lecture, the student needs to dedicate 2-3 hours outside of class reviewing material. For example: 12-18 credit hours = 24-36 hours per week of study time.

Study Prep:

- Study daily (reinforces knowledge)
- Calculate study time
- Complete assignment/link concepts (connect maps)
- Consider a study group
- Bounce/Share ideas/Quiz each other
- Discuss/Organize your studying:
- Rewrite notes/Use index cards
- Highlight/Use post its
- Study looking for similarities/differences

Tip: Review the front of the NCLEX book, it provides strategies on how to approach NCLEX styled questions.

WOW..... THAT FIRST EXAM!

Many students are disappointed in the results of the first exam. Nursing exams are not like exams taken in previous academic courses. Nursing exams are developed to test not only knowledge but critical thinking, decision making, prioritization, and safety.

Nursing education prepares the generalist nurse. The goal of programs is to prepare a competent nurse at a general level. Many students are concerned about experience in a specialty. Although you may later assume a position in a specialty, state boards are primarily preparing a generalist nurse.

There are many sources available that will assist the student nurses in strengthening their ability to pass an NCLEX styled exam. There are apps, index cards, and quizzes available both online and in paper form for studying. The benefit to exposure to NCLEX styled questions is the fact that it provides you with rationale.

Tip: Review an NCLEX review book to learn about NCLEX questions, and learn ways on how to approach them.

WHAT IS SKILLS LAB?

Skills labs are an important part of nursing education. The primary goal of most skills' lab is to enhance the students learning and exposure to concepts with the opportunity to practice in a laboratory setting. The skills lab is where the nursing student can practice the skills that are used most often, seen, or expected in practice.

The skills lab is unique as it combines the atmosphere of the clinical setting with learning technology. The skills lab may have various learning stations. Static manikins with movable limbs, safety equipment, IV pumps, oxygen delivery, crash carts, medicine carts, feeding pumps are items you may see to name a few.

Examples Skills:

- Intravenous (IV) catheters/Injections (muscular, subcutaneous, and intradermal)
- Nasogastric Tubes/Feeding Pumps
- Foley Catheters/Wound Care
- Health Assessment Models
- Suction Equipment/Oxygen Therapy

PREPARING FOR SKILLS LAB

Skills lab is huge because often times students are not able to actually perform many of the skills learned in lab on a live patient until after they have graduated from the nursing program. It is a good idea to review the organ system, or understand the purpose for a specific skill. For example, for a catheter going into a bladder, it is a good idea to review the anatomy and physiology of the urinary system. Consider reasons why a patient may need to have a catheter inserted for long term or short-term use.

Pre-Lab Prep:

- Watch videos/read assigned articles
- Ask about open lab times/ Practice if possible
- Review the planned skills (available in the textbook)
- Complete any learning activities before the lab

During the lab:

- Be prepared/ Do not be late
- Maintain Safety/Expect to see complex equipment
- Treat experience like it is a real situation

WHAT IS SIMULATION?

Simulation is a teaching technique that develops the ability of an individual to solve problems. It is called simulation because it mocks an actual clinical environment. Simulation uses static and simulated manikins in a safe controlled environment. Some colleges/universities may use real people (standardized patients).

Simulation may be used to assess several types of learning. Cognitive (knowledge), kinetic (skills and actions), affective domain (dynamics, and feelings) may be tested. Safety, decision making, attention to detail, situational judgment, and critical thinking (thought process) are also evaluated. It can also provide an opportunity for the student to self reflect and for the instructor to provide feedback.

Simulation has become a major part of the nursing students' learning experience and varies across programs. Simulation may be used individually, in teams, or done virtually. For some programs, simulation accounts for 50% of student clinical time.

Many of my previous students have verbalized disdain for simulation. There are several reasons for this. First, in simulation there is a fear of the unknown. Second, there is no way to practice for simulation. Third, in simulation things do not go as planned or expected. All bummers for students.

PREPARING FOR SIMULATION

Simulation can be difficult. However, there are strategies that can improve simulation success. Simulation is individualized and varies. Typically there are three components 1) pre-brief, 2) participation, and 3) debrief.

Pre-brief is usually done prior to the simulation. Pre-brief may include the following; review of learning objectives, orientation to the learning environment, overview of learner expectations, and completion of pre-read (prep work). The pre-brief establishes the standards.

Active participation is expected. That means several things: 1) participate in the pre-brief. , 2) Review the policies and procedures of the simulation, 3) Orient to the simulation area, 4) Make sure you are aware of the learning activities, 5) Be familiar with the rules, equipment, & environment, 6) Exude confidence, and don't panic!

Debrief occurs after the simulation and provides an opportunity to reflect and discuss the simulation. Students should reflect honesty on the scenario. Simulation may be evaluated cither formative (not graded) or summative (graded). Faculty may be measuring: confidence, satisfaction, reflection, course objectives, and understanding.

WHAT IS CLINICAL?

Clinical is the component of the nursing program in which students actually utilize all of the skills learned in the classroom, lab, simulation in the real live clinical environment. The amount and type of clinical required varies across programs.

Clinical rotations times are varied and may range from 4 to 12 hours. Timing depends on the program, course, accreditors, and the clinical site. Clinical may include day, pm, or night shift schedules. Clinical rotations may also be scheduled with a group of students or with a staff nurse preceptor. Some clinical allow students to rotate off of the primary unit to observe other specialty areas.

Typically, clinical becomes increasingly more complex as the student moves forward. Clinical rotations can take place in a variety of settings from community to trauma to non-profit clinics. Each is an opportunity to learn and become acclimated to the profession.

In clinical the theory (knowledge), laboratory (skills), and simulation (application of knowledge) are applied in the clinical environment with real live patients. Clinical is where it all comes together. Clinical is vital to nursing education and has been recognized as the heart of nursing education.

PREPARING FOR CLINICAL

Being prepared for clinical is the best thing a nursing student can do. Clinical experience is vital. The day before requires preparation. Preparation means that the student be well rested and prepared to work.

Recommendations Include:

- Preparing your uniform/dress professionally
- Eat/pack a lunch/snack
- Setting an alarm- plan to arrive early (15-30 minutes)
  Be prepared for pre-conference
- Present with necessary supplies/equipment

Your instructor will discuss expectations. After clinical you should reflect on the day, document accomplishments, experiences, and review your accomplishments against the grading rubric and course objectives. This will provide the student with a good depiction of how they are progressing in the course. Remember clinical is the best opportunity to get acclimated to the role of licensed nurse.

Tip: Preparedness is vital to your success! Always be Prepared!

THE CLINICAL START

Clinical instructors, professors, nurses, and clinical sites have varied expectations. There are strategies to assist in being organized in the clinical environment. The nursing student should always try as much as possible to understand the expectations and to have a working plan when in the clinical environment. Your instructor will guide you.

Strategies:

Familiarize yourself with the patient disease/diagnosis, understand the patient's problem, map out or determine the plan of care. Then ask yourself:

- What is the overall plan?
- What goals are we attempting to reach?
- What other team members are involved?
- What is my plan for the day?
- How can I best organize and manage my time?
- What is my role (plan and interventions)?

Tool: Free Document Clinical Start Guide in Dr. Dixon's Toolbox

COMMUNICATION

Effective and therapeutic communication is a huge part of nursing. **Communication** helps to establish a rapport, enhances patient engagement, and can build professional connections. Communication goes two ways and is an exchange of information. Communication requires one to listen and hear and has verbal and non-verbal components.

Key Points:

- Don't be afraid to ask questions/clarify doubts
- Own up to your mistakes
- Be able to locate policies and procedures
- Document often
- Perform assessments

The following is recommended with patient interactions acknowledge, introduce, discuss duration, explain and say thank you. AIDET® was developed and is patented by the Studer group.

Tip: Always use therapeutic and effective communication.

PROFESSIONALISM

Professionalism is expected in the field of nursing. Professionalism is more than your outward appearance. Professionalism in nursing includes a variety of personal qualities and behaviors that demonstrate commitment to effective performance in the role of nurse. The manner in which you present, act, communicate, and execute are key.

There are several components of professionalism. In the role of the nurse examples include, but are not limited to showing compassion and respect for others; responding appropriately to the emotional response of patients and family members; demonstrating a calm, compassionate, and helpful demeanor, and being supportive. Being committed and confident, responsible and dependable; honest and ethical; and being present are central professional characteristics.

The American Nurses Association has a Code of Ethics which discusses the manner in which the nurse conducts themselves as members of society. This is hugely important. Just remember, this is your responsibility. Professionals have a responsibility to monitor themselves

SAFETY

Safety is a necessity in today's complex health care environment. Safety should be executed with in day to day operations and in care delivery at all times. Safety is the responsibility of many. However, the nurse has his/her own responsibility in maintaining safety.

Patient safety is the cornerstone of high-quality health care. Patient safety is exhibited when a nurse uses all strategies to prevent avoidable errors and patient harm.

Safety Measures:

- Improve the accuracy of patient identification
- Utilize clear and effective communication
- Implement safe medication administration
- Monitor medications for high alerts
- Reduce delays in treatment
- Provide equitable services
- Establish safety systems in every interaction
- Access and follow policies and procedures
- Conduct safe admissions/discharges/transfers
- Maintain competence through education

CRITICAL THINKING

Critical Thinking is a type of problem solving and/or decision making. Critical thinking encompasses the ability to make reasoned judgments that are logical and well thought out. It is the type of thinking that is systematic, logical and is based on facts. This level of thinking also allows for the ability to question and to reflect on the process of reasoning. This is done to ensure safe practice.

Thinking critically requires the nurse to ask why or why not, look for patterns, and/or themes, and make a decision. Critical thinking is self-directed, self-disciplined, self-monitored, and self-corrective. Nursing instructors in the classroom and clinical environment assist students in developing the skills necessary to critically think. This is often achieved through assignments, exams, quizzes, case studies, simulation, discussions, concept maps, and care planning.

Tool: Free Concept Map Template located in Dr. Dixon's Toolbox

STUDENT SUCCESS STRATEGIES

Nursing students absorb a large amount of content, work under a great deal of stress, have enormous responsibilities, and expectations. Remember, you are being prepared to enter a profession that is important, and highly valued by society. Below are tips for student success.

Things to Note:

- Know your scope of practice
- Practice with safety in mind
- Your instructor is an advocate, a resource, and can be a professional reference

Successful Students:

- Present attentive, professional, and respectful
- Are organized/set a schedule/take notes
- Get adequate sleep/rest
- Ask questions and/or clarify
- Spend adequate time studying

Everything in life has some risk, what you have to actually learn to do is how to navigate it....

— REID HOFFMAN

Chapter Four

STEP FOUR.... NAVIGATING

Nursing programs has several primary goals. The first is to develop strong nurses based on a curriculum that enhances knowledge, skills, and abilities. The next is to have students successfully complete the program within the expected time frame. The third is to prepare students to complete the National Council Licensing Exam (NCLEX) and obtain a license upon program completion. This chapter describes the NCLEX, provides tips on how to approach NCLEX styled questions, and provides recommendations on NCLEX preparedness.

WHAT IS NCLEX?

The National Council Licensing Examination (NCLEX) is the national exam that all nurses take to attain licensure. It is provided by the National Council of State Boards of Nursing (NCSBN). The NCLEX exam uses multiple choice, computer-based methods to test the minimum competency required to practice nursing safely.

There is a website that provides a vast amount of information about the NCLEX. That includes exam questions, provides a test plan, discusses test taking, and detailed components of the exam. The website also provides information on 1) pre-exam- what you need to know; 2) Registration- how to sign up; 3) Exam day prep- tips, and 4) After the exam- what you need to know. The NCLEX test plans are reviewed every three years. Check the NCLEX Test Plan website for further details.

WHAT ARE NCLEX QUESTIONS?

NCLEX questions are types of questions that you will find on the national licensing exam. NCLEX practice exams are available for practice and provide a look and feel of the NCLEX exam. The practice exams are made from a variety or previously used NCLEX exam questions.

The National Council of State Board of Nursing has practice exams available on their website for a fee. The exams are for both the LPN and RN exams. Each is available in English and French versions. There are also many books available that describe the NCLEX exam and ways to be successful approaching these types of questions.

There are also NCLEX review books. Reading the front of the NCLEX review book walks the student through the NCLEX test taking strategies. NCLEX review books are available for purchase on Amazon. Practice questions may be in the form of Books, Apps, On-Line, or video.

Tip: Plan to review NCLEX styled questions prior to your first exam.

CONQUERING EXAMS!

There is a basic rule of thumb for studying. For every 1 credit hour of course load, the student needs to dedicate 2-3 hours outside of class reviewing material. For example: 12-18 credit hours= 24-36 hours per week of study time.

Study Tips:

- Implement adequate study time (as above)
- Study Similarities and Differences
- Consider a study group/study buddy
- Rewrite notes/Use index cards
- Highlight/Use Post-Its
- Create concept maps on major diseases/disorders
- Create and review drug cards
- Review and understand NCLEX questions

Tip: Review the front of the NCLEX book, it provides strategies on how to approach NCLEX styled questions.

Tool: Concept Map Template located in Dr. Dixon's Toolbox

NCLEX STUDY PLAN

It is a good idea to create strategies to successfully pass the NCLEX exam. There are review programs, books, online modules, quizzes, and courses that can be taken too assess the students knowledge prior to the exam. The most highly recommended plan from students is to establish your own individual plan. Faculty and instructors also recommend that nursing students expose themselves to NCLEX styled questions and review the rationale that is provided with each of the questions.

NCLEX study plans may be developed based on organ systems by major content areas. Each student should be able to reflect and understand areas of weakness. If labs are an area of weakness or the cardiac system (for example). Then additional time should be devoted to these topics or content areas.

Tip: Develop an individual NCLEX Study Plan
Tool: Free NCLEX Sample Study Plan is provided in DR. Dixon's Toolbox.

PREPARING FOR NCLEX

Successful completion of the NCLEX exam is vital to obtaining licensure. Reviewing, reading, and exposure to questions will allow the student to learn of their individual weaknesses. NCLEX questions provide rationale. Review books, apps, and flash cards all help you to establish a baseline to identify areas that need improvement. NCLEX styled questions may be answered on a computer, tablet, or smart phone.

Recommendations: It is recommended that you plan to take the NCLEX exam within the first 90 days of program completion. The student should create a NCLEX study plan to begin reviewing months before sitting for the exam. Increased exposure to NCLEX styles questions has been known to better prepare the student for the board exam.

Tool: Free Sample NCLEX Study Plan is located in Chapter 8-Dr. Dixon's Toolbox

PASSED NCLEX, NOW WHAT?

Successful completion of a nursing program and passing NCLEX is a huge step. It is a time to celebrate and embrace this time. Create memories, prepare/plan next steps, and reflect.

Create Memories: Take nursing and or graduation photos. Have a party, plan a vacation and enjoy family. Create a memory book, scrapbook, journal your experiences.

Preparing/Planning: Work on your Resume and portfolio. Gather the documents to complete these two items. Develop job search strategies, cast a wide net. Don't be afraid to explore.

Reflect: Think about all of your newfound knowledge, and the experiences you have gained. Remember why you entered the profession of nursing. Reflect on your successes.

Tools: Resume Guide and Portfolio Development Tool located in Dr. Dixon's Toolbox

By failing to prepare....you are preparing to fail....

— BENJAMIN FRANKLIN

Chapter Five

STEP FIVE...PREPARING

Nursing is a profession. As with many professions one must be prepared. Nursing programs have expectations prior to entering the profession and those involve as a member of a team. A huge component of preparing for entry is how you present yourself professionally. That includes having the ability to document your learning, maintain professionalism, and tell your story. Preparing for entry into the nursing profession requires a few steps along the journey.

The student nurse or new graduate nurse has either successfully completed or is planning to soon sit for the NCLEX. This is also a time that the student should preparing to tell their individual story. I recommend that these not be taken for granted. This chapter provides tips on resume building, portfolio development, and discusses interview questions.

THE RESUME

Your resume should provide a succinct but detailed and informative description of each of the health care activities and responsibilities you have gained. Your resume should tell a story about how you are qualified for the role you desire. Your resume is your brand. Make it special!

A compilation of documents which exemplifies your skills, qualifications, education, training, and experiences, and professional affiliations. A hard copy is beneficial to provide to a potential employer as it showcases your individual accomplishments. It may give you an edge on the competition and can be used as a guide or reflection during an interview.

Tool: Free Resume Development Guide located in Dr. Dixon's Toolbox

THE PORTFOLIO

The portfolio is a compilation of documents which exemplifies your skills, qualifications, education, training, and experiences, and professional affiliations. The portfolio has several benefits. First, a hard copy can showcase your individual accomplishments to a potential employer. Then, it may give you an edge on the competition. Finally, it may be used as a guide for conversation during an interview.

A portfolio should be presented in a professional, organized binder. Preferably the binder should be tabbed. Sheet protectors are recommended for protection. There are several options that may be placed in the portfolio. These items need to be presented in an orderly fashion. These items should be updated as you matriculate through the nursing program (students) or nursing career (licensed nurses).

Tip: The portfolio is an awesome way to display your skills, talents, and professional growth.

PORTFOLIO DEVELOPMENT

Items to include:

- Resume/Vitae
- Personal Accolades/Awards
- Professional References (3-5) from (Managers/Supervisors/Previous Professors)
- Letters of Recommendations
- Exemplar Work/Projects
- Academic Recognition/Honors/Deans List
- Transcripts/Course Completion/Education
- Clinical Evaluations (work or academic)
- Professional/Scholarly Activity
- Certificates/Licenses
- Conferences/Seminars/Presentations
- Memberships/Committee Involvement
- Volunteer Experiences/Community Service

Tool: Free Portfolio Development Tool located in Dr. Dixon's Toolbox

THE INTERVIEW

There are key components that one should consider prior to scheduling an interview. The new graduate must be able to discuss the knowledge, skills, and abilities attained in the nursing program and how that has prepared them for the role for which they are applying.

Documents To Include on Portfolio:

- Resume/Vitae/Certificates
- Transcripts/Diplomas/Licenses
- Clinical Experience
- Professional Development/Presentations
- Community Involvement /Volunteering
- Professional Reference/Recommendations

Interviews May Be Rendered:

- In Person/Phone/Skype
- Individually/One to One/In groups

Tip: Ask a professional such as a mentor, or instructor to conduct a mock interview and provide feedback.

PREPPING BEFORE THE INTERVIEW

There are a number of consideration and task that need to be considered and done prior to the interview. There is often completion for jobs. Particularly for new graduate nursing positions. You need to ensure that the jobs that you are applying for align with your own. Below is a list of some things to do prior to the interview.

Check the organizations website:

- Review the organization/Drive By
- Read the mission, vision, and values
- Know the overarching philosophy
- Do each of these align with your own?
- Human resources/Assess Benefits
- Review the job description
- Assess parking/safety

Prepare the following:

- Portfolio (includes resume)
- Briefcase/Carrying Case/Folder
- Interview attire/Interview questions

POSSIBLE INTERVIEW QUESTIONS

Interviews are designed to assess the potential employee/employer relationship (to see if you would fit in). Interview questions may come from variety of areas. Below are possible questions and includes the purpose.

Credentials- To verify credentials

- How long were you at?
- What knowledge do you have?
- What qualifies you to perform in this role?

Experience- To subjectively evaluate background

- What did you learn?
- What skills match the position?
- What could you contribute to the organization/unit?

Situational/Opinion- To determine response in a situation/scenario.

- What would you do in this situation?

- Tell me about a time when you have had to work or deal with a problematic situation?
- Please provide some examples of how you overcame....

Competency/Skills- To align past skills with specific competencies required for the position.

- What is your experience or knowledge of?
- Are you familiar with?

Behavioral/Reflection- To objectively measure behaviors as a predictor of future results.

- Can you tell me about a time when you?

Personality- To determine how you self-reflect.

- What is your worst attribute?
- What would you say are your strengths?
- What items would you improve on?
- What do you perceive as a weakness?

Tip: Never reflect negatively on previous experiences. Interview questions should be answered with a positive spin.

QUESTIONS YOU SHOULD ASK

During an interview a standard question is to be asked by the potential employer, "Do you have any questions for us?" Below is a list of the questions you may want to consider. This shows your interest and your thought process.

Orientation:

- What is orientation like?
- How long is orientation?
- Ask about transition to practice programs.
- These are programs that support the transition of the student nurse to the role of the licensed nurse.
- Usually the first year of practice

Typical Day:

- Can you describe what a typical day looks like?
- How do you measure success in this role?
- What is the most challenging aspect of this job?

Culture:

- What is the culture of the organization/unit?
- What is the best part of working here that I could not see on a tour?

Growth:

- Are there opportunities for professional development?
- What are common career paths?
- What is the performance process like?

Follow Up:

- When do you anticipate filling this position?
- When can I expect to receive follow up information?
- When will a decision be made?

Final Question:

- If you have a moment, I would like you to review my portfolio?
- Is there anything else I can provide that would be helpful?

CONSIDERATIONS AT THE OFFER

You need to either formally accept or decline the offer professionally. If necessary ask for an extension on the time to make a decision. Review job description and weigh the pros and cons. Whether you accept or decline do so professionally.

Items to Consider:

- Advancement
- Tuition Reimbursements/Benefits/Perks
- Time off/Schedule/Flexibility
- Commute
- Health Insurance
- Retirement/401K
- Vacation/Sick/Personal Time

Tip: Compare the salary after you have reviewed the total benefits package. Is it worth it? Find out if the compensation package is negotiable.

Any transition is easier if you believe in yourself and your talent....

— PRIYANKA CHOPRA

Chapter Six

STEP SIX...TRANSITIONING

Transitioning into the role of the licensed nurse does not come without some serious concerns. The roles and responsibilities of the student nurse are far less then the role of the licensed nurse. Both roles are important. Remember the student role allowed for someone to guide, support, and facilitate learning. The licensed nurse is preparing to work more independently and make critical decisions for patient care. Although this process evolves it is referred to as transition to practice and is an important part of entry into the profession.

The transition to practice piece can be a difficult time for newly licensed nurses. This transition can be exciting, scary, frustrating, and enlightening. However, there are plans that assist the new nurse often called orientation or internships. Either way, it helps to recognize the importance of a good transition. This chapter describes tips, strategies, and recommendations helpful for this transition.

TRANSITIONING

Upon program completion the nursing student transitions into the practice environment. The truth is with all the knowledge learned in the student's program of study. The actual environment, coupled with responsibility, complexity of patients, rules, regulations, and expectations is vastly different than the nursing program. Nursing has recognized this as a concern. Therefore, internships, orientation, and transition programs have been put into place.

The National Council of State Boards of Nursing (NCSBN) has conducted research and realizes the importance of supporting this transition from student nurse to practicing licensed nurse. In fact, the NCSBN has developed booklets that welcomes new graduates to the profession. For more information on transition to practice seek the following resource: **Transition To Practice**

KNOWING THE REGULATIONS

There are several websites that the licensed nurse must be aware of that describes regulations. Understanding these regulations ensures that you have knowledge needed to function in your role. Review is recommended.

The Nurse Practice Act provides information on the rules and regulations that guide and govern nursing practice. The National Council State Boards of Nursing (NCSBN) has a website to locate your states nurse practice act located at: **Nurse Practice Act**. There is also a **Nursing Code of Ethics.**

The State Board of Nursing for your state will provide the scope of practice and other rules and regulations for the profession. This may be located by placing "state board of nursing" for (your state) in a google search.

Patient Safety is a huge component of safe practice. A popular framework utilized in healthcare is Team Strategies and Tools to Enhance Performance and Patient Safety. Team STEPPS is an evidence-based framework to optimize team performance across the healthcare delivery system. Team STEPPS may be found at: **Team STEPPS.**

ORIENTATION

Orientation can be overwhelming. Nursing school covers the basics. In nursing school you have that licensed nurse to oversee your actions. After nursing school, you become an independent thinker and your responsibility and independence becomes a reality.

Orientation times vary from a few weeks to several months. Specialty areas may have a longer orientation period. Orientation is unpredictable, so expect the unexpected. Preparation, planning, organization and patience is key during this time. Organizations spend lots of money on training for new roles.

Tip: Orientation should meet your needs. Be your own advocate.

NAVIGATING ORIENTATION

Navigating orientation is a good idea. You are responsible for understanding your orientation. Below are items to consider.

Orientation Is a Time to Learn:

- The organization/environment (work flow)
- Staff, nurses, managers, or health care team members
- Policies, procedures, and processes
- How to plan, prioritize, and organize care
- Documentation/Electronic Health Record
- What you don't know

Recommendations:

- Take one day at a time/Set realistic goals
- Observe and participate as much as you can
- Find a good support system
- Listen to the experienced nurses

Tip: Orientation should meet your needs and you should feel comfortable once completed.

WHEN ORIENTATION IS OVER

When orientation is over an additional transition occurs. The transition after orientation involves independent thoughts and actions. The licensed nurse has a great responsibility to the patients, families, the organization in which you work and society. This is where all that you have learned from education and experience comes together to provide competent and safe care.

This is a great time for transition for several reasons. This is a good time to reflect upon newfound knowledge. The nurse should feel the ability to provide competent and quality patient care while working as a member of the healthcare team. This is a time to be excited and positive. One thing to note is that you will not know everything. Remember, you have resources. I have not met a nurse in my years of working and teaching that knows everything.

Tip: Know who and where your resources are and utilize them!

THE ACTUAL CLINICAL ENVIRONMENT

The clinical environment can be overwhelming. Please note, the environment in which you will work as a licensed nurse is very different than the environment you were exposed to as a student nurse. Knowledge of the environment and knowing how to function in the environment is critical.

There are several items to be aware of. First, know your education has prepared you with the knowledge, skills, and abilities to practice with competence and confidence. Second, regardless of experience you will be exposed to new things. Third and finally, know that nurses do not work in silo. Work with your colleagues and learn from others.

Tip: This is the licensed nurses time to shine. Shine bright like a diamond!

FIRST DAY PUNCTUALITY

You passed the program, you completed the degree, you passed your boards, you made it through several phases of the interview. This is not a time for self-doubt. "You got this"! Be confident. Tips are below.

Pre-Arrival:

- Review key info into related specialty
- Review on-boarding info
- Be prepared for the first day: (bandage scissors, pen light, watch with a second hand)
- Clipboard for documents
- Bring and complete all necessary paperwork

Arrival:

- Come in a little early
- Smile (never let em see you sweat)
- Get settled and be ready to go
- Expect Introductions

FIRST DAY PREPAREDNESS

The first day on your own can feel intimidating. Just like your first day of nursing school. This time you have way more knowledge and experience. Preparation is huge.

Preparation begins well before your shift starts. Arriving at work is only the beginning. How you manage from the start is huge. That is why, obtaining your assignment, and completing some self regulation and monitoring is vital to success.

Report and Assessment:

- Listen/Ask questions/
- Complete full initial assessments
- Round frequently

Self-Regulation and Monitoring:

- Identify gaps in skills/Always practice safely
- Document as you go/Communicate clearly

NURSING NEWS YOU CAN USE

There are certain things that all new graduates should know. The list that was created below is helpful news the new grad can use. Listed in no particular order. Just helpful!

- Chart as you go- If it isn't documented it isn't done
- Know... that you will not know everything
- Work is not like nursing school
- Learn and practice delegation
- Stay engaged and develop professionally
- Document your accomplishments
- Being overwhelmed is normal in the beginning
- See one, Do one, and Teach one
- Create your own identity (you are like no other)
- Get to know and communicate with doctors
- Take your break
- Smile... It's contagious
- Familiarize self with equipment
- Review policies and procedures
- Work with the educator, preceptor, be a team player

BUILDING BRIDGES THROUGH NETWORKING

Nursing is a profession in which bridges are built. Building bridges means making connections and creating professional relationships. Connections are made through networking. Networking helps nursing graduates find new positions, discover new specialties, and share knowledge.

Networking comes in two primary forms professional and strategic. **Professional networking** allows you to develop relationships within your field. These may be done in person, online, or through an organization. **Strategic networking** is when deliberate connections are made when the nurse is searching for a career or trying to define a career goal. This is most likely to occur when a nurse is considering a change. In both cases developing relationships, making professional connections and remaining professional is key.

Tip: Establish relationships and build bridges

ESTABLISHING BOUNDARIES

There are professional boundaries that should be maintained as a member of the nursing profession. Boundary violations occur when a nursing professional has a personal, professional, or business relationship with a patient. These situations should be avoided. A professional relationship must be maintained whenever possible.

The Nurse Should Avoid:

- Engaging in flirting
- Spending too much time with a patient
- Displaying favoritism
- Reviewing records when not assigned
- Establishing personal or business relationships with patients.

SOCIAL MEDIA WARNING

Social media is another area in which boundaries need to be established. Social media should not be used as an avenue to violate a patient's rights, privacy, or confidentiality. Remember nurses have a legal and ethical obligation to maintain confidentiality.

The Nurse Should:

- Never transmit information on social media
- Never share or post images about a patient
- Never disseminate information that may lead to patient identification
- Do not take photos on personal devices
- Report confidentiality breaches
- Be familiar with organizational policies
- Do not post content regarding employer without permission

Tip: Be aware of social media policies.

DEALING WITH DOCTORS

Medical doctors (MD)s are not your friend. Medical doctors are also not the enemy, they are professional colleagues. There should always be a collaborative nurse-physician relationship. There is an expectation of effective communication.

Effective Communication:

- Present organized, logical, and concise
- Be prepared before calling the MD- Provide the situation, background, assessment, and recommendations (SBAR).
- Know the nursing process. A-Assessment, D-Diagnosis/Data Gathering, P-Planning, I-Intervention, and E- Evaluation (report)

Strategies:

- Be prepared/Be confident/Not apologetic
- Don't allow emotions to get involved
- Be your patients advocate when necessary
- Report negative behavior
- Be patient and establish a rapport with the physicians

PROFESSIONAL DEVELOPMENT

The purpose of professional development is to increase knowledge, improve skills, expand learning, or enhance capabilities. Due to the complexity and changes in health care it is expected that nurses remain current in practice. Professional development is the process of improving practice through continual development and lifelong learning.

Document:

- Conferences/Education (formal courses)
- Informal opportunities situated in practice
- Certifications/Degrees/Licenses
- In-service education
- Presentations
- Committee/Memberships/Affiliations
- Experience

Professional Development Can:

- Enhance knowledge, skills, and abilities
- Enhance interpersonal communication skills
- Improve technological skills

LICENSED NURSE RESPONSIBILITIES

Each day in the life of the RN is different. Actions, attitude, and activities are based on the organization, patient flow, acuity, environment, and colleagues. None of which are easy to control. The one thing you can control is to manage your responsibilities.

Nursing Responsibility:

- Take ownership/Be accountable
- Educate yourself/Practice self-care
- Provide consistent quality care
- Organize/Plan/Lead
- Support another nurse/Lend a helping hand
- Stay healthy/Take time for yourself
- Invest in comfortable shoes, uniforms, clothes
- Embrace change. Change is inevitable

THE ORGANIZED NURSE

Nurses that are more organized are typically more productive. Organization allows the nurse to manage time more effectively. Being organized also makes a better overall impression. This recognition could result in increased responsibilities or even promotion to leader.

Nurses that develop organizing tools will increase the likelihood of success. Based on observations from working with students, colleagues, as well as my own professional practice experience there are various tools to assist with organizing. Nurses should either invest in or create these tools.

I along with many previous students personally love the collapsible clipboards manufactured by: Collapsable Clipboards website and also available for purchase on Amazon. The clipboard allows you to hold multiple documents, folds in half, and can fit in the pocket of a scrub top or lab coat/jacket.

Tip: Organization helps with time management.

Becoming is never giving up on the idea that there's more growing to be done.
   Michelle Obama

Chapter Seven

STEP SEVEN...BECOMING

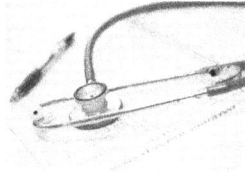

There comes a time in the career of a nurse when you become the nurse you set out to be. When the nurse becomes, there may be a change in direction, one may take on a new role or a fresh start, work outside of your comfort zone, or just follow your heart.

It is my belief that becoming occurs during different times in a nurses career. Often the nurse has dedicated years into the profession and begins to come into his/her own. A certain grit develops, the nurse becomes empowered, confidence is gained, truths are uncovered, and a sense of control occurs. For some this takes years or even decades.

This chapter discusses change. Then, it highlights some of the controversies that occur during an individuals development as a nurse. Next, it uncovers some significant issues within the profession. Finally, options and recommendations are provided on how to become a success.

THE NEED FOR CHANGE

Our experiences inform what we become, how we evolve, and the changes that we allow as members of the profession. One thing that is certain, change is inevitable. The process of becoming allows us to personally grow and change. Some nurses seek change and can't wait function in a new role. Others may resist change or may feel stuck.

Change involves a realization of your own potential. The current role you are in may not be your permanent. This change may be inevitable as you recognize a desire to contribute to the profession in another way.

Sometimes the role you find yourself in is comfortable. Some days can be more difficult then others. Some roles in nursing come and go. On occasion you will know that your days are numbered. If you are considering a change, speak with others in a similar role. These nurses can provide helpful advice and insight. Remember as a licensed nurse, you have many options.

Tip: Don't be afraid of change

MAINTAINING COMPOSURE

Maintaining your composure is helpful in any profession, especially nursing. Nurses work in highly stressful and emotionally draining environments. Stress may come from workload, environment, difficult patients/families, stressful situations, or colleagues.

Some environments may be difficult to work in. These issues make it difficult to maintain your composure. Nurses must practice maintaining composure within the various health care environments. Remember the environment can be stressful.

Maintaining Composure:

- Step away/take a walk
- Find your happy place
- Take a minute
- Slow down/Take a deep breath
- Reflect on the situation
- Be strategic/Pray
- Separate yourself
- Adopt a positive attitude/Develop a social network
- Don't rush/Take a guilt free lunch/Limit caffeine

AVOIDING A TOXIC ENVIRONMENT

History dictates that "nurses eat their young" and recently there has been a term introduced called "lateral violence". In both cases it is said that nurses are not supportive of each other and Do NOT do well collaborating as professionals. These types of actions contribute to a toxic environment.

Resolving toxicity:

- Be realistic/Redirect behavior
- Be non-judgmental/Acknowledge feelings
- Document issues/Create a plan to overcome
- Assess and report uneven workloads
- Identify who is contributing to the behavior
- Meet with the manager
- Become a change agent
- Lend a helping hand to another nurse
- Make the environment better
- Know your organizational policies

Tip: Realize you can't change others, only yourself.

AVOIDING BURN OUT

There will be times when you experience burn out as a nurse. The nursing profession is very rewarding. It can also be very stressful, creating burnout. No worries... this can be fixed.

Examples of Burnout:

- Fatigue/Lack of focus
- Weight loss/Weight gain/Hair loss
- Stressed Out/Anxiety/ On edge
- Lack of sleep (insomnia)/Need to get away

Relief Measures:

- Take your scheduled breaks/Learn to say no
- Focus some time on yourself
- Consider reducing your workload
- Take some time to relax
- Stay healthy/Get adequate rest
- Meditate/Track your activity level
- Plan a vacation/Get a massage
- Develop a new hobby
- Create outside connections

OH, THE POSSIBILITIES

Nursing has a myriad of possibilities. Nursing offers various degree levels, program types, and career options. Each of these options provides new opportunities. Experience is gained in every aspect of nursing. Take some time to consider the possibilities that are available in nursing.

Nursing Possibilities

YOUR CONTRIBUTION

As a nurse you are contributing to the profession of nursing. You probably have sent many years dedicated to serving others. Nurses hold a unique place in the health care system. Your role is valuable. Your contribution to nursing does not end at being a licensed practicing member of the profession.

Valuable Ways to Contribute:

- Recruit others into the profession (peers, family)
- Be an advocate
- Provide education
- Collaborate with other professionals
- Write a book
- Patent an idea
- Coordinate community outreach
- Volunteer in the community
- Join a nursing association
- Share health information

NEVER BURN BRIDGES

There are bridges that we cross to get to the next path. Remember bridges are pathways. What you need to know is that the nursing profession is not a place to burn a bridge. It is a great chance that if that bridge helped you cross; you may need that bridge again.

Recognize the Following:

- It is small world/Protect your reputation
- Never say never/Learn to forgive and let go

Build Bridges:

- Follow up when using someone as a reference
- Stay connected/build relationships/say thanks

Looking Back on A Previous Job:

- Don't speak negatively
- Plan your exit/Give proper notice

Tip: Never Burn Bridges

WORDS OF WISDOM FROM DR. DIXON

Words of Wisdom:

- Never allow anyone make you feel incompetent.....
- On time is late... Be early.... Be prepared....
- Treat others how you would want to be treated...
- Own up to your mistakes...
- Seek the good in people.....
- Make your own judgments....
- Commit to developing a better you........
- Keep an extra uniform nearby......
- Be positive... never let them see you sweat...
- Plan for the unexpected...
- Invest in lifelong learning....
- Never profess to know everything.....
- Stay current with evidence-based practice...
- Learn something new...
- Smile... It's contagious
- Contribute to the Profession/Then Self Reflect
- Be ready for change it is inevitable
- You reap what you sow....

AFTERWORD

The topics in the Journey to Becoming a Nurse guide has provided a multitude of items the nursing student, practicing nurse, and experienced nurses could use.

This guide has illuminated new information unveiling fresh ways to approach the profession of nursing. The Journey to Becoming a Nurse was written to assist nursing students, new graduates, and licensed nurses about the challenges and realities of practice. Knowledge is Power and Experience is the best teacher.

It is the hope of Dr. Dixon that this guide will allow nurses entering the profession within this Journey to becoming a Nurse, a Step by Step guide to encourage nurses into the profession and provide them with the knowledge they need to be successful in the profession.

Thank you for reading please share with your colleagues.

THE BUTTERFLIES

The butterfly is a deep and powerful representation of life and transformation. The butterfly is also seen as a symbol of freedom and resurrection. When I think of my previous students I think of the butterfly. Something special that we see fluttering around along our journey to becoming.

My previous students have inspired me, gave me a reason to get up and go, encouraged me to keep teaching, and have made me realize the importance of recognizing that we are all different. I have created an image in the form of a butterfly. The names (first only) are of my previous students. I am sure at my age, I missed some but please know your impact. Each of these students had contributed to me as a professor and a person. Thank you! Blessings to you all and Be well!

Lourdes
Olivia
Nancy Maritza
Jesse Shaun
Danielle
Deidra Kelsy Sakura
Christian Carmen
Katherine Rochelle
Lorena Caleb Samantha Darlene
Amber Julie Keshonda
Celest
Jennie Rebecca Kendra
Austin
Anne
Joseph Stephanie Asl
Edith Tricia
Jane Lora Erin
Heather Haley Pat Ellie Gwe
Laura Melinda Sharon Ama
Monique
Marton Ron Belinda Kristen Ja
Jaimie
Marwah Jes
Christina Michelle
Nektaria Sarah Jessie Brenda Alyssa
Lady Kelsey Laurel Angel
Araiana Vanessa Ericka
Kelly Yasmin
Alycia Corina
Alter Angela
Kassidy Gea
Suzanne Patricia
Morgan

Colin
Ashleigh
Christine Michael
Susie
Griselda Marisol Arnoldo
Brianna
Alexandra Dedra Hannah April
Valerie Cynthia Emily Kathryn
Erica Dunstan Meghan
Courtney
Maria Amelia Khara Renuka
Tim Ahsan
Erika Suytry Tiana
yJennifer Amy
Jenna Kimberlee
Crystal Iryna Revie
Diana Alexander
da Angie Paris Tanesha
Ang
ca Megan Yaritza
Nevine Stacie Abigail
sa Melissa Gean Gianna
Puneeth
icole Shane Jonericson Ariel Sheena
Loretta
Annise Alicia
Brittany Isabel
Edward Herrera
Ryan Joel
Isaac

Chapter Eight

DR. DIXON'S TOOLBOX

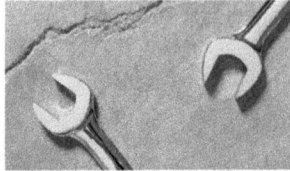

This chapter contains documents that have been shared with previous students and nursing colleagues. In fact, nursing students, transitioning RN's, licensed RN's, and fellow nurse educators have indicated that they are useful. They are provided for your reference. Contents include:

    Nursing Program Search Tool
    Clinical Start Guide
    Concept Map Template
    Concept Map Sample List
    Resume Writing Checklist
    Portfolio Development Guide

DR. DIXON'S TOOLBOX

These tools may be helpful depending on where you are in your journey. The main idea is to provide them to you as a resource for current or future use. Listen if it doesn't help you, maybe... just maybe.. One of these tools can help someone else. So, if you think any of these tools can help someone else.....Please Share!

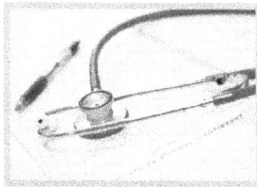

Dr. Tonya Dixon

Program Name	Program Name
Program Location	Program Locat
Program Type LPN, RN, BSN, BSN Accelerated	Program Type LPN, RN, BSN,
Accredited	Accredited
NCLEX Pass Rates	NCLEX Pass Ra
Program Length	Program Lengt
Education Model Face to Face/Hybrid/On-LIne	Education Moc Face to Face/H
Admission Requirements	Admission Req
Admission Deadlines	Admission Dea
Waiting List	Waiting List
Financial Cost	Financial Cost
Support Services Financial Aid, Scholarships, Job Placement, Tutoring	Support Servic Financial Aid, S Placement, Tu

	Program Name
	Program Location
erated	Program Type LPN, RN, BSN, BSN Accelerated
	Accredited
	NCLEX Pass Rates
	Program Length
-LIne	Education Model Face to Face/Hybrid/On-LIne
s	Admission Requirements
	Admission Deadlines
	Waiting List
	Financial Cost
ps, Job	Support Services Financial Aid, Scholarships, Job Placement, Tutoring

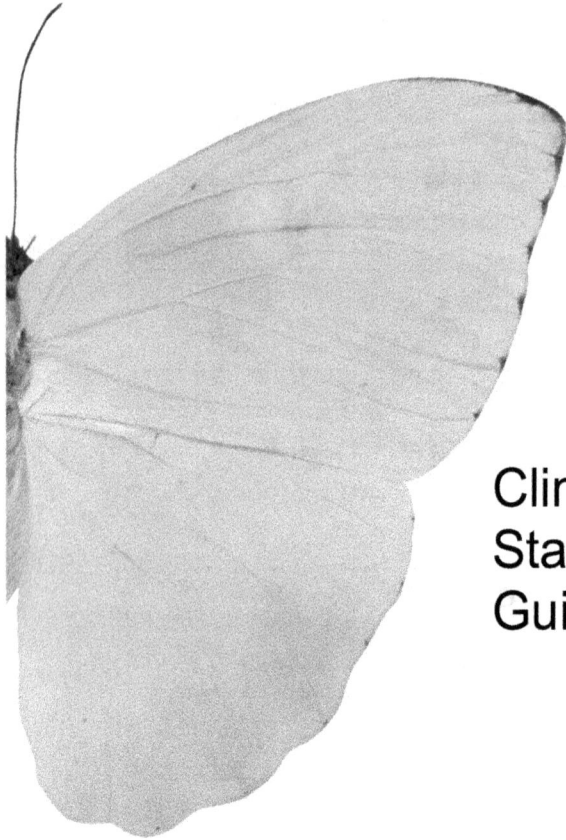

Clinical
Start
Guide

Dr. Tonya Dixon Ed.D, MSN, MBA, MPH, RN

GET STARTED RIGHT AWAY

- Attend Pre-Conference
- Go to the unit and get report on your assigned patient(s) (write it down)
- Log into the system and obtain the patient history and review current meds
- Connect with nurse/preceptor
- Review Chart/Electronic Medical Record (EMR) for pertinent/relevant information
- Plan out a schedule for the day
- Make sure care and meal is provided work with patient care tech
- (PCT) or Certified Nursing Assistant (CNA) to coordinate.
- Obtain full vital signs on your assigned patient (includes pain assessment)
- Complete your head to toe assessment on your assigned patient
- List medications and begin drug cards
- Determine the patient problem and initiate care plan, begin to write assessment
- Within the first two hours, connect with instructor for verbal report and review of plan
- Plan on lunch being flexible
- Plan charting, write up assessment
- Complete follow up assessment/charting and or medications
- Plan a concept map, care plan, other assignments for possible submission
- Post conference

LOOK GREAT EVERY TIME

- Remember to be professional and communicate with members of the team
- If your patient is going for a test or OT/PT if possible, go with (ask first)
- If the doctor comes in the room (don't leave) stay and listen
- Review the chart, assessment findings, and plan then piece together the clinical picture

COMMUNICATION IS KEY

- Report off to preceptor, instructor whenever you go to break or lunch
- Give report to another student nurse (practice)
- Ask instructor/preceptor for best method of contact /(usually via phone)

Dr. Tonya Dixon

What Are the Nursing
Interventions?

Disease

Patho

What is the Medical
Management?
Treatment?

Ris

der

gy

Signs
&
Symptoms

How is Disease/Disorder
Diagnosed?

CONCEPT MAP BOOK

Medical Surgical

2020
DR. TONYA DIXON
Concept Maps

Cardiac/Circulatory:
- Congestive Heart Failure
- Coronary Artery Disease
- Cerebrovascular Accident
- Myocardial Infarction or Angina
- Hypertension
- Anemia
- Shock

Respiratory:
- Chronic Obstructive Respiratory Disease
- Asthma
- Cystic Fibrosis

Digestive/Gastrointestinal (GI):
- Appendicitis
- Cirrhosis
- Diarrhea or Chron's
- Pancreatitis
- Peptic Ulcer

Excretory/Genitourinary (GU):
- Chronic Kidney Disease
- Cystitis
- Incontinence
- Kidney Stones

Nervous:
- Alzheimer's Disease
- Meningitis
- Multiple Sclerosis
- Parkinson's Disease
- Seizure Disorders
- Migraine

Endocrine:
- Type I Diabetes
- Type II Diabetes
- Thyroiditis
- Hyperthyroidism

Allergy and Immunology:
- Angioedema
- Anaphylaxis
- Sinusitis
- Bronchitis
- Allergic Rhinitis

Integumentary:
- Psoriasis
- Dermatitis
- Ringworm
- Alopecia

Musculoskeletal:
- Osteoarthritis
- Rheumatoid Arthritis
- Bursitis

Reproductive:
- Amenorrhea
- Menopause
- Prostate Cancer
- Preeclampsia

Eye/Ear/Nose/Throat:
- Glaucoma or Cataracts
- Conjunctivitis
- Macular Degeneration
- Otitis Media
- Sinusitis

Other Diseases/Disorders:
- Obesity
- Insomnia
- Sarcoidosis

Psychological Disorders:
- Schizophrenia
- Bipolar
- Depression
- Anxiety
- Attention/Hyperactivity Disorder

Infectious Diseases:
- Bronchitis
- Candidiasis
- Common Cold
- Influenza
- Herpes Simplex
- HIV and AIDS
- Measles
- Tuberculosis
- COVID-19

MONDAY	TUESDAY	WEDNESDAY	
4	5	6	7
Hematology/Immune 75 Q's	Hematology/Immune 75 Q's	Hematology/Immune 75 Q's	Re Cl
Advanced Directives	Advocacy	Case Management	
11	12	13	1
Neurosensory 75 Q's	Neurosensory 75 Q's	Neurosensory 75 Q's	M
Ethics	Informed Consent	Information Technology	Q Q
18	19	20	2
Gastrointestinal 75 Q's	Gastrointestinal 75 Q's	Gastrointestinal 75 Q's	E
Health Promotion &	Psychosocial Integrity	Psychosocial Integrity	Pl
25	26	27	2
Maternity 75 Q's	Pediatrics 75 Q's	Psychiatric 75 Q's	Ps
Pharmacological & Parenteral Therapies	Pharmacological & Parenteral Therapies	Pharmacological & Parenteral Therapies	R Pc

20

FRIDAY	SATURDAY	SUNDAY
1 Cardiovascular 75 Qs Review NCLEX test Plan	**2** Cardiovascular 75 Qs Prioritization Assignment/Delegation	**3**
8 Respiratory 75 Q's Interdisciplinary team	**9** Respiratory 75 Q's Confidentiality/HIPAA	**10**
15 Musculoskeletal 75 Q's Safety and Infection Control	**16** Musculoskeletal 75 Q's Physiological Adaptation	**17**
22 Endocrine 75 Q's Physiological Integrity	**23** Endocrine 75 Q's Pharmacological & Parenteral Therapies	**24**
29 Comprehensive Review Exam	**30** Comprehensive Review Exam	**31**

Study Plan (2020)

Resume Writing Checklist

Your resume should provide a succinct but detailed and informative description of each of the health care activities and responsibilities. Your resume is your brand. Make it special!

Format

☐ Don't use more than two 8½ × 11" pages, except for those in exceptionally high-level positions where resumes might be up to four pages.

☐ Maintain plenty of white space. Avoid long paragraphs of text.

☐ Use bullet points for ease of reading.

☐ Select a clear, easy to read font.

☐ Be consistent with text alignment.

☐ Use bold or italic to draw the reader's eye to key points.

☐ Use a pre-formatted template in Microsoft Word.

☐ Search for examples and play around with formatting.

Style and Structure

☐ Depending on the job you're applying for, the style can be formal or slightly less so. However, the wording should remain 100% professional.

☐ Use high impact, positive words to make for compelling reading.

☐ A good resume should flow in logical order: contact details, summary statement, experience starting with your most recent job, education and training.

Contact Details

☐ Include your phone number, email address, and LinkedIn profile. Ensure your email address is professional. Do not use college/university email address.

Summary Statement

☐ The summary statement is your sales pitch. State why you should be selected for this particular role, with a clear match of your skills to the role applied for.

Education and Training

(If you are a student, place this section before your employment history.)

☐ List your education and training in reverse chronological order.

☐ Include all formal education post-high school.

☐ Detail all certificates, qualifications, and additional education.

Resume Writing Checklist (Page 2)

Experience

- ☐ List your experience/employment history in reverse chronological order.
- ☐ Highlight key responsibilities and accomplishments.
- ☐ Back up your achievements with figures, percentages, and data where possible.

Clinical Experience

- ☐ Document your clinical experiences. Track your clinical hours. Indicate the unit you gained experience on. Describe the clinical experiences you obtained during your nursing education on the various units or within the organization.

Professional Accomplishments

- ☐ Document your professional development such as certificates, licenses, courses, conferences, and presentations.
- ☐ Document professional growth leadership such as presentations, awards, academic and or professional accolades.

Document Community/Social Involvement

- ☐ Document your involvement with volunteering, mentoring, community service, professional or student organizations.

Document Skills

- ☐ Document your level of knowledge regarding the electronic health record (various types) for which you have familiarity (examples: Epic, Cerner, Sunrise).
- ☐ Experience with Microsoft Office such as Word, Power Point, and Excel.

Document Linguistics

- ☐ Document your skills regarding fluency in another language.

Keywords

- ☐ Many employers use computerized systems to sift through resumes during the initial application stage. Include industry/company/job relevant keywords and phrases to ensure yours passes these tracking systems to move onto the next stage.

Proofread

- ☐ Spell and grammar checks are essential. Use Spell check. Get a few other people to read over your resume to be 100% sure everything is correct.

PORTFOLIO DEVELOPMENT

Sample Cover Sheet

JANUARY 1, 2020
DR. TONYA DIXON
Professional Portfolio

Portfolio Development Guide

This template can be used as a checklist for documents you will place in your professional portfolio. Always keep original documents. Make copies of the most important ones. Store these separately, such as in a safe deposit box. Sections may be divided by experience, community involvement, professional development, awards/accolades. Below is a list of documents recommended for your portfolio.

Document
☐ Transcripts
☐ Certificates
☐ BLS/ACLS/PALS Certificates
☐ List of References (3 Professional)
☐ Reference Letters
☐ Licenses
☐ Accolades (Deans List)
☐ Awards/Accomplishments/ Acknowledgements
☐ Volunteer Certificates/Work
☐ Copy of Resume/Vitae
☐ Evidence of Community Involvement
☐ Degree and Diploma Certificate or Status
☐ Copy of Resume or Curriculum Vitae
☐ Continuing Education
☐ Professional Development
☐ Copies of Stellar Evaluations
☐ Documentation of Involvement In Committees
☐ Articles
☐ Newsletters
☐ Performance Evaluations
☐ Memberships in Professional Organizations
☐ Awards/ Other Recognition
☐ Presentations
☐ Documented Leadership

Dr. Tonya Dixon Portfolio Development Guide (2020)

ACKNOWLEDGMENTS

I would like to express gratitude to previous students and nursing colleagues who encouraged this writing. My previous students taught me the value of knowledge sharing particularly of experiential knowledge. Nursing colleagues have encouraged me to be myself, to love nursing, and to do it with compassion. Blessings to you always! Thank you to my Beta readers and advanced copy readers for feedback and recommendations.

Dr. Tonya Dixon Ed.D, MSN, MBA, MPH, RN

ABOUT THE AUTHOR

Dr. Tonya Dixon resides in Illinois with her husband. Tonya has 15 years of experience teaching students seeking nursing degrees. Students connect with her after completion and thank her for sharing her knowledge, for her dedication to the profession, and education.

Tonya's first publication was her completed dissertation which was based on a mixed-methods study focused on the preparedness of the undergraduate registered nursing student in clinical education. Tonya remains immersed in clinical facilitation through teaching, writing, and blogging. Tonya loves educating and encouraging the growth of aspiring health care students, nurses in the profession, as well as nursing educators.

Dr. Dixon is currently developing a book to support nursing faculty who teach future nursing students. Coming soon, The Innovative Education for the Next Nursing Generation, a facilitators guide to optimal clinical learning. Learn more about Tonya @ Doctor-Dixon.com or The Consultants Circle